EXPLAINING
De-Greecing the Church
The impact of Greek thinking on Christian beliefs

DAVID PAWSON

ANCHOR RECORDINGS

First published in Great Britain in 2017 by
Anchor Recordings Ltd
DPTT, Synegis House, 21 Crockhamwell Road,
Woodley, Reading RG5 3LE

**For more of David Pawson's teaching,
including DVDs and CDs, go to
www.davidpawson.com**

**FOR FREE DOWNLOADS
www.davidpawson.org**

**For further information, email
info@davidpawsonministry.org**

ISBN 978-1-911173-20-5

Printed by Lightning Source

Contents

This booklet is based on a talk. Originating as it does from the spoken word, its style will be found by many readers to be somewhat different from my usual written style. It is hoped that this will not detract from the substance of the biblical teaching found here.

As always, I ask the reader to compare everything I say or write with what is written in the Bible and, if at any point a conflict is found, always to rely upon the clear teaching of scripture.

David Pawson

PART ONE

We used to live in a small village in North Hampshire called Sherborne St. John – about a thousand souls. There was one huge mansion in the village. As you might guess, that is a National Trust house, a Tudor brick mansion owned by the Soames family until the National Trust took it over. It is a beautiful old building with large windows and mellow bricks, but at some stage in its history the Soames family stuck onto the main front facing the lake a Greek portico. Here you have these Corinthian columns with the triangular pediment above, and it looks totally out of place.

It offends me deeply whenever I see it, whoever stuck that on. It took me back to Geneva. When I visited Geneva I wanted to see St. Peter's Church where John Calvin's reformation took place. St. Peter's Church was of course a medieval Catholic Gothic structure with soaring archways and buttresses – a typical old Gothic building. Inside it is very bare because Calvin got rid of all the decoration, all the statues, all the carvings, and replaced all the elaborate decoration with simple pews. So it is nothing much to look at inside. But when we came out of the west door, to my horror, against this beautiful Gothic church, again has been stuck on (I can only say "stuck on") a Greek portico. Again, you have the columns and the triangular pediment above, stuck on to a Gothic building. It doesn't even fit; it looks terrible. As I backed off across the square to get a better look at this monstrous carbuncle (to quote somebody else) I came across a statue on a plinth at the other side of the little square. On the statue is the bronze figure of a man recoiling in horror as he looked at this Greek portico. Underneath, it said "Jeremiah". You know, I was quite unable to find out who had put the statue there or why, and how he got away with it. There are no picture postcards of it. I wanted to get a photograph of this bronze of a prophet recoiling in horror at the Greek addition to what had been an attractive Gothic church, but it is very awkward to do so. It is a parable, and I identify with that statue.

I recoil in horror at what Greek thinking has done to the Christian Church over centuries. Immense damage has been done to the Christian faith right up to today. I want to show you that you and I have been victims of it, even reading the Bible with a pair of Greek spectacles on. So the meaning of my title (and you might have thought I couldn't spell; the meaning of "De-Greecing") is precisely what I have said: that we need to get out of the Church the Greek influence that is alien to the Church, alien to our faith. Now of course most people are aware that the Greek has had some influence on our culture. Those who think the foundation of Western civilization is Judaeo-Christian are mistaken. It is far more Graeco-Roman. Let me just pick out at random four aspects of *our* modern culture, *our* Western life, that go straight back to Greece.

The first aspect I want to draw attention to is the architecture. Until steel and reinforced concrete were available to architects we had to build mostly with stone. When you look at all the public buildings that have been built of stone you are looking at Greek temples. Walk around the City of London, look at the Exchange, look at St. Paul's Cathedral. Particularly since the Great Fire of London in

1666, which destroyed a couple of hundred churches – Sir Christopher Wren rebuilt them on the basis of Greek architecture. All Souls Langham Place is thoroughly Greek as you will see if you ever go and worship there. You walk around and look at the Wren churches in London – you are looking at Greek architecture. Whether the columns are Corinthian, Doric or Ionic it is Greek through and through. We have based our architecture on them. Town halls, museums, libraries, art galleries – up and down the land you will find them.

Even more in America. Walk around Washington DC, look at Congress, look at the memorials. They are all Greek temples. Look at any large house in America and you will find the front of it is a Greek temple. So architecture owes a very great deal to Greece. Now I am not saying that is wrong at this stage; I am just pointing out how deeply their architecture has influenced our lives.

Let us move on from that to politics. There is not a trace of democracy in your Bible. Every country in the Bible was an absolute monarchy ruled by a king. It was a true kingdom – not like the United Kingdom, which is neither united nor a kingdom, but a true kingdom in which the king rules, in which there are no political parties, in which there are no elections, no votes, no debate about laws. The king makes them and that's it. That is what every country was in the Bible, and the Bible doesn't teach democracy. I remember going to see the film "The Ten Commandments". Cecil B. DeMille came on at the beginning to make a speech and he told us that this film was about the beginning of Western democracy: the story of Moses. There is not a thing about democracy in Moses' story or the Ten Commandments – but there it is.

We are now used to democracy. So Winston Churchill was right when he said, "Democracy is the worst possible kind of government, except all the others." What he meant was that it is safe from dictatorship when you can change this lot and put another lot in. Though as Studdert Kennedy said about a general election: "It's one lot of sinners out and another lot in." Not only did the Greeks start democracy, it is to them we owe an idea called "devolution" – constantly pressing outwards and pressing down the opportunity for people to govern themselves. But none of this is in the Bible.

A third aspect of our life today is sport. Where *did* we get our love of sport, our *obsession* with sport? I might even dare to say for many men in this country the *religion* of sport? It didn't come from the Bible; the Bible has very little about sport. The only text that springs to mind is, "Bodily exercise profits little". A friend of mine said he got all the exercise he needed climbing hospital stairs to visit his friends who had been jogging! Where did we get sport from? We got it from Greece, from the Olympic Games, and just over the Aegean Sea, the Ionic Games in western Turkey. Sport was an obsession of the Greeks. The cultivation of the body came from Greece. Their statues tell you the ideal physique to have, and greatly exaggerated biceps and so on. The display of the human body was part of Greek culture, which is why most of their sports were played in the nude.

Let us take a fourth aspect: entertainment. The Greeks had everything we have got on television – except television. They had theatres, they had debates and discussions. They lived for leisure. They did not live for work. Work was a necessary evil, but you found your true meaning of life in leisure after you had finished your work. If possible, you employed a slave to do your work so that you could be a gentleman of leisure, so that you could pursue the interests of leisure.

Whether it be in the great libraries they built, or in the sports stadium which I have mentioned, or in the theatres, or in the debating chambers, or the open air debating places like the Areopagus, Mars Hill, where Paul joined in a debate, or tried to speak. They were entertained; they had to be. The leisure industry had to be a gigantic industry. Two-thirds of the people in Greece were slaves to do the work so that the rest could enjoy their leisure.

Now do these things sound vaguely familiar? We are a people of sport; we are a people of leisure; we live for the weekend. We find our real being in the activities that *we* choose in our spare time rather than in the activities that are chosen for us in our work. But I am concerned not so much about the influence of Greece upon our general culture, but about the subtle influence of Greece upon the Church and upon Christian thinking, which is perhaps hardly noticed by many.

The root of Christianity is in quite a different world from Greece. Your Bible tells you where our roots are. Our roots are in the Hebrew world – the Jewish world. That world was almost the opposite in every respect of ancient Greece. The Old Testament is totally Hebrew and was actually completed before the Greeks appeared on the scene. The more you read the Old Testament the more you study the roots of Christianity, which were way down in the soil long before Greece was thought of, though it is mentioned just once or twice in the Old Testament. The Hebrews did not live for leisure. They worked a six day week, and the seventh day was not a holiday, it was a holy day, a day for God, not a day for *them*. They lived for work and for worship. They did not live for sport; they didn't have time for it. They didn't live for leisure. They worked for God and they worshipped God.

The New Testament, it is true, is written in the Greek language. But every writer bar one was a Hebrew. Though the language is Greek, the thought is Hebrew. It is still a Jewish book. The one Gentile writer, Dr. Luke, got all his information from Jewish people and travelled with a Jewish propagandist called Paul. So our whole Bible is Hebrew from beginning to end, and that is why, for example, the Bible has a very high view of work, and in particular a high view of *manual* work, whereas for the Greeks manual labour was for the slave and for the immigrant. The hard labour of the hands was not for the Greek. It was for anyone else they could get to do it. Does that strike you as familiar in modern Europe? If you have got a German car it was probably built by people who were not Germans.

Manual labour is considered down the scale in Greek society. People who work with their heads are higher up the social scale than those who work with their hands. In the Bible it is the other way on. In the Bible, manual labour has the top dignity. Most of those whom God called to full-time service and to great work had already qualified in some form of manual trade, whether it was shepherd or fisherman ("tax collector" was an exception). The Son of God himself was put into a carpenter shop for eighteen years. He was a woodworker for eighteen years and a wonder worker for three, and if my mathematics are right, that is a ratio of six to one, which is the same as his Heavenly Dad. Isn't it? Read Genesis 1 lately? Eighteen to three, six to one. Fancy putting the Son of God, the Saviour of the world, to work with his hands for eighteen years as a preparation to save the world! It is the last thing that the Greeks would ever have even *thought* of doing, but it is very Hebrew.

Now here we have two completely different worlds which developed quite independently of each other, though not too far away from each other geographically, just a few hundred miles across the sea. The Old Testament was completed by 400 BC. Though the canon, or recognised collection of books of the Old Testament, was not settled until about 100 BC, nevertheless by 400 BC the last word of our Old Testament had been written – before the Greeks came on the scene.

Malachi was the last prophet to bring a word from God. For the next four hundred years God was totally silent. It was the second time he had been silent for four hundred years. The first time was when the Hebrews were slaves in Egypt. But the second time was between our books Malachi and Matthew. For four hundred years God didn't send a prophet and didn't speak, which is why we don't have any of the books written during those four centuries in our Bible. There were Jewish books written, and we call them the Apocrypha or "the hidden books", but they don't come in our Bible because they are not *God's* Word. They are human words; they are true – true history, true ideas, but they are not God's Word. It is fascinating that there is one phrase which occurs 3,808 times in the Old Testament but not once in the Apocrypha. It is the simple phrase "Thus says Yahweh", or in your Bibles "Thus says the Lord". That phrase does not occur for four hundred years, nor do any miracles occur for four hundred years. It is almost as if God withdrew from the earthly scene for four hundred years.

Speculating, I think that is when the devil seized his chance. Within decades of God having spoken his last word, Greek philosophers were striding onto the world stage and giving us *their* philosophy, *their* thoughts, *their* words. Very quickly we had Socrates – almost immediately after Malachi. He was followed by his pupil Plato, and later followed by Aristotle, the tutor of Alexander the Great. These three men in particular gave us a whole new idea, a whole new ideal.

That word "ideal" is characteristic of them. So these philosophers gave us new ideas, and new ideals. Socrates wrote nothing, did all his teaching in dialogue with his students – question and answer all the time – concentrated on logic and ethics. All of them were concerned about moral behaviour, about how you make bad people good, in simple terms. But Socrates was condemned to death. He was accused of corrupting the youth and of being an atheist. He was condemned to commit suicide by drinking hemlock. But as he drank the poison he discoursed to his students about the joy of dying, about the release that it would bring.

However, Plato his pupil did write a lot, poetry and prose, and opened an academy in Athens to which students came from all over the then known world. Then Aristotle, the third of the great three, wrote four hundred books. The teaching of these three men has spread right through Europe and through Western civilisation, and has had a profound influence on all of us whether we like it or not. Without even being conscious of it, the Greek influence came to us through our normal education.

Now these three men were fathers of Greek *philosophy* and that word simply means the way people think. They also profoundly influenced their culture. But I am going to draw a distinction now between the Greek culture, which I have already mentioned and Greek philosophy, which is my major subject. The Bible says, "As a man thinks in his heart, so is he." In other words, the way we are constantly thinking is going to shape our behaviour, our character and our lifestyle. The way we think is the key to the people we are – both as individuals and in society. The way we think about ourselves, the way we think about the world in which we live, the way we think about the God above, all these will shape our character, shape our lifestyle, make us what we are.

I want now to concentrate on the one particular aspect of Greek thinking which has corrupted the Christian faith more than any other. It is in the realm of ideas and ideals. When you have ideals you have values. Everybody has values – but when we have values we have a scale of values, a kind of ladder. At the top we put those things we value most highly, and at the bottom those things we least value. We finish up with a scale of values, and everyone has such a scale.

If I just asked you to make a list, if your house was burning down what would you go back into the house and bring out? That would reveal immediately what is at the top of your scale of values. I will tell you now what I would go back for: my Bible. Not because I am terribly pious, but because it contains years of notes and underlining, and all the fruit of my thought for years and years, and I just couldn't be without it. I would run back in for that (well, my wife first). What would you run in for? What is your scale of values? What would you be most willing to lose in your present lifestyle, or what would you want to hang on to like grim death?

The Greeks, those philosophers, taught a scale of values and this was it. Imagine a ladder. The top rung we may label "spiritual". They put spiritual things as the highest value of all. The bottom rung we would have to label "physical", because they valued physical things least of all – we are talking about the philosophers now. Where would they put mental and intellectual things? They would put them probably on the second top rung, very close to the spiritual. But can you begin to see what is happening? A gulf is opening up between the spiritual and perhaps the mental, and the physical down below, and though it was intended simply to be a graded scale of values it developed into what we call a "dualism", which means a sharp division of life into two compartments, one of which you value highly and the other of which you hardly value at all. It became a split between the spiritual and the physical, and once you have made that kind of a division then all sorts of other things follow from it.

You begin to divide a person up into two parts: body and soul. It is amazing how many people think Christians do this. But it is a Greek idea that I have a soul in a body. When God breathed into the body of dust that he had made, the body of clay, he breathed into the dust and Adam became a living soul. People think that means that God put a soul into the clay. No it says, "The *clay* became a living soul." That phrase "a living soul" may be found in Genesis 1 applied to animals – the same phrase. Animals are living souls because in Hebrew thinking a soul is a breathing body. It is not something distinct *from* the body; it is a live body, a living breathing body.

That is why when your body was in danger (using the traditional distress signal) you didn't call out "S.O.B!" you shouted out "S.O.S!" – "save our souls". What you really mean of course is keep my body breathing! Now you are thinking Hebrew. But the idea that we are made up of two parts, the body, which has little value, and the soul, which has real value, has led to Christians talking about saving souls when we are really called to save *whole people* – to save their living bodies as well. See how that changes your thinking.

Let us take a typical Christian song which is thoroughly Greek. "John Brown's body lies a-mouldering in the grave. John Brown's body lies a-mouldering in the grave. John Brown's body lies a-mouldering in the grave and his *soul* goes marching on." That is not what Christians believe; that is what Greeks believed. But it is astonishing at how many Christian funerals people talk like Greeks.

Not only is man divided into body and soul but life gets divided into sacred and secular. I had an ex-missionary come and talk to me in church the other day. I said, "What are you doing now?"

He replied, "I've gone back to engineering. I'm in a secular job again."

I said, "No you're not."

"Yes," he said, "I am. I was a missionary but now I'm an engineer again."

I said, "You're in a sacred calling." He looked at me as if

I was, well, from another planet.

I said, "There's nothing secular except sin. All work ranks the same to God."

I'm going to come back to this, because *we* tend to divide people into those who have a sacred job and those who have a secular job. That is Greek thinking. There is no such thing as a secular job. There are immoral jobs and illegal jobs. They are secular. But Got would rather have a good taxi driver than a bad missionary. I wonder when you last realised that. I am coming back to that later. It is one of the areas in which Greek thinking has ruined our Christian thinking about the work that we do.

Life is divided into sacred and secular; the universe is divided into natural and supernatural – which is not a division you find in the Bible. Let me just ask you a question: would you put the devil on the natural or the supernatural side of the universe? You see, the Bible doesn't talk that way. The Bible talks about Creator and creature. Now which side is the devil in *that* one? He is a creature. But as soon as you think Greek you put him on the supernatural side alongside God, and that is the wrong category for him.

Then we divide religion between heaven and earth, between eternal and temporal, and this gulf seems to open up. Death then becomes a friend rather than an enemy. In the Hebrew Bible death is an enemy from beginning to end because death is a restriction. You lose your body at death and that restricts you. From now on you cannot communicate with the living. From now on you are shut off from those you love. It is a restriction, an enemy. It breaks up families. But to the Greeks death was a friend. Go back to Socrates drinking hemlock and saying, "I'm about to be released from the prison of my body."

Let me try to illustrate this. Imagine a glass of water. To the Greeks the glass is my body and the water is my soul, and my soul is imprisoned in my body. It needs release. When I die it is as if somebody takes the glass of water, pours the water back into the ocean, and smashes the glass on the rocks. I am released from my body. My soul flows back into the ocean of reality. The trouble is that it loses its identity. The water doesn't know who it is then. It is lost.

Yet the Greeks looked forward to death as a friend – as a release from this prison body. I have heard that said at many funerals – "What a merciful release", as if the person is out of all suffering. They could actually have gone into worse suffering, but it looks like a release because the muscles relax and the body is at peace. But death is a restriction. It is an enemy. The Old and New Testaments always treat it as the enemy: the last enemy we fight, and the one which wins, the one who needs to be conquered by God. The good news is that death has been conquered by Christ. But it is an enemy. It is not to be welcomed – ever.

It is not even a natural event; it is an execution for all of us. This body that I am using will one day rot, because I want to be buried not cremated. It will become a stinking horrid mass that you won't want to look at, touch or smell. Why does it do that? Because a rotten person has lived in it. It is God's sentence on people who are rotten: that their bodies rot. Which is why he said, a thousand years before Jesus came, that, "If ever a holy man lives on earth I will not leave his body in the grave to rot," which is why Jesus rose before the fourth day.

Now let us go back to these Greeks. There are two major effects of what we call this "dualism" – this division between sacred and secular, temporal and eternal, physical and spiritual. This deep gulf has effects on two major questions of life. Number one: *good* and number two: *God*. This dualism has affected Greek thinking about what is good and who is God. Let us take the idea of "good" first. If you value spiritual things very highly and physical things very lowly aesthetically, it is not long before your aesthetic values change into moral values.

I could give you a good example here: Sunday clothes. Sunday clothes could be purely aesthetic. But I was brought up to believe you were sinning if you didn't get on your Sunday clothes, and aesthetic values slipped over into moral values. It is one of the hardest things for us to distinguish between: what are aesthetic and cultural values, and what are genuine moral values? They get confused.

The result of the Greek thinking on the good was that people began to think spiritual things were good and physical things were bad. You can see where that would lead. It would lead to a belief that your body was the source of evil and your soul was the source of good, and that the task of your soul was to get free of the evil influence of your body; that it is because we live in a physical world with physical bodies that there is evil all around us; we need to be set free from the physical in order to be good. Now that is a most *dangerous* idea, but I am afraid we're going to see that it's got right into Christian thinking. Yet it is *Greek thinking*.

When they thought about God they put him up there in the spiritual as far away from the physical as possible, and therefore they split the Creator from his creation. They could not believe in a God who would get entangled in this physical world, a God who would have anything to do with it. He had washed his hands of it. He is *spiritual*. He is way up there; he is in an eternal world far removed from this changeable world of time and space, this physical world in which we live. Now that leaves a problem. If God is far above all physical things and never soiled his hands with physical things, who created all *this*? They came up with two rather funny answers. I give them to you because you will see the point of them later.

The first answer was to believe that there was a kind of demi-God, what we call a "demiurge". It is a funny word. It means a kind of half god, someone in between God and the world. They postulated this being somewhere halfway between who was responsible for creating and sustaining the physical universe, but God himself was way above it all. He had a kind of deputy, an agent who soiled his hands with a physical world for him and on his behalf. That was one answer.

The answer that Aristotle came to was that the world was never created at all, that matter is eternal, that the universe was always here, and that it manages itself. Interestingly enough, Aristotle was the first man to teach the theory of evolution. The universe, being eternal, controlled itself and evolved itself. It is quite independent of God. That idea wasn't to surface until over two thousand years later through a man called Erasmus Darwin, Charles's grandfather, who was a thoroughgoing atheist and believed the same as Aristotle, and taught his little grandson Charles the theory of evolution.

In what I have been sketching very briefly and in-adequately – simplistically, really – I think you can detect the beginnings of secular humanism. The foundations were laid in Greece for secular humanism today. The world in which we live is the world of privatised religion in which you can be religious as a private matter, but don't expect it to impinge on public life at all. It all began way back there.

Now I want to trace the history of the interaction between the Greek and the Hebrew world, and after that I am going to go through some examples of Christian thinking in particular areas where we have been seriously misled by Greek thinking. Finally, I want to tell you how to counteract this, how to cure yourself of it, how to de-Greece yourself, because we are not going to de-Greece the Church unless we de-Greece the members of the Church. The Church itself doesn't exist apart from us, and so it is we who need to be de-Greeced.

But first I want to give you a very quick historical sketch of how these two worlds met – the Greek and the Hebrew worlds – and what happened when they did meet. We will go right back to BC, and we need to focus on two cities in the ancient world where they met. One was Jerusalem and one was Alexandria in Egypt. Let us take Jerusalem first. There came to Jerusalem one day an invader, a Syrian king, called Antiochus Epiphanes, or Antiochus IV. He came charging down from Syria to invade the little land of Israel and capture the capital. Antiochus Epiphanes was sold on Greek culture, and he was determined to impose it on every land he conquered. So he imposed Greek culture on Jerusalem ruthlessly, and the story is terrible.

He built a sports stadium and introduced nude sports, which could hardly be more offensive to the Jewish people. He went into the Temple and erected a statue of Zeus, the "king of the gods", on the high altar. Then he sacrificed pigs – pork – on the altar. Not roast lamb, roast pork. Then he brought temple prostitutes into the Jewish temple and filled the vestries of the priests until they became a brothel. It took him three and a half years. In those three and a half years the Jewish people were raped in every sense of the word. It was a terrible time. It had been prophesied by the prophet Daniel centuries before, and he had called it "the abomination of desolation" – this dreadful imposition of Greek culture on the Jewish people, the first real encounter they had with it.

Just as an aside, Jesus picked up both Daniel's prediction and Antiochus Epiphanes' three and a half years. Jesus spoke about a future time of distress such as the world had never seen that would happen before the end of time. That would be what came to be known as the Great Tribulation, which would last three and a half years, forty-two months, 1260 days. It is all there in the book of Revelation, a kind of future event foreshadowed by Antiochus Epiphanes – the Abomination of Desolation. The reaction among the Jews was utter horror.

There were two groups who reacted very strongly. One was a family of seven brothers called the Maccabees. They decided to fight. They fought a terrorist campaign and managed to get rid of the Greeks, and for many years had their own Jewish king again—the Hasmonean Dynasty, which lasted until 63 BC when the Romans came.

The other group that reacted against this invasion of an alien culture was a kind of Puritan movement; they called themselves Pharisees. They were going to live separately from all this. They would not go to the theatre; they would not go to the stadium. They were going to live separately and keep themselves pure and clean. That is how the Pharisees began, who turned out to be Jesus' greatest enemies at one stage. But there it was. It is all history. Now that was the first encounter between Greek culture and Hebrew culture. That is how it finished.

It was a failure – to impose that culture on the Jewish people. But turn now to the city of Alexandria on the Nile Delta in Egypt, and here, in a much more subtle way, the Greek influence came not into their culture but into their thinking, because by now Jews were being scattered around the then known world, the Mediterranean coast, into the Diaspora, the dispersion. Jewish students were coming to the second greatest Greek university in the world. The first was Athens, the one that Plato had started. The second was Alexandria, started by Alexander the Great, Aristotle's young pupil. He opened a university in Alexandria, built a new city, and to it there came Jewish students then, later, Jewish scholars.

Here was a point, a melting pot, where Jewish thinking and Greek thinking mixed in the same school, the same lecture theatres, the same university. Who would win here? Who would influence whom here? Well, it was right here in this Alexandria university that the Jewish scholars decided to translate their scriptures into Greek so that the Greek world could hear the truth about the God of Israel. Seventy scholars translated faithfully the Old Testament into the Greek language. It is called the "Septuagint", after the seventy scholars who did it. Or sometimes you see written in Roman numerals "LXX", shorthand for the name of this Greek translation. So that was good. This would enable the Greek world to hear about the true God, the only God, the God of Israel.

But I am afraid the influence also went the other way and a new method of Bible study was introduced to the Jewish people, which you will hear in Christian pulpits every Sunday today. It is called the *allegorical* method of Bible study. What it means is that there are hidden spiritual meanings in every part of the Bible; that the simple plain sense of the statement is only one meaning and that behind it there is a spiritual meaning. Especially the physical statements of the Bible must have a spiritual meaning behind them to be of real value.

So they began to read the Bible not just in its plain, simple, literal physical statements, but they began to look behind it for a hidden code. That began a way of looking at the Bible which leads right through by a single thread, straight through, to a book called *The Bible Code*, by a man called Drosnin. I bet you have heard of that one because you have seen it in bookshops and stationers. The Bible, according to this approach, is coded – full of secret messages; full of very spiritual things. Though it may make a simple statement about a physical fact, the real meaning is behind all that – so this is an allegorical approach to Scripture.

Now clearly there are some parts of scripture that are allegorical, that are symbolic. But most of scripture is in plain, straightforward statements which need to be taken at their face value. If you are always looking for some hidden message, some hidden meaning, the big problem becomes that there is no control on what you find. You say, "Well this is what *I* think it means," and somebody else says, "Well, I think *this* is what it means" – and who is to say who is right? You can then read *into* Scripture what you want to find. That is called *eisegesis*, instead of reading *out* of scripture – which is called exegesis – what is already there.

A man called Philo began to do this with the Old Testament and introduced it to his fellow Jewish scholars. He grasped that Greek doctrine of a demiurge between God and the world, who created the world – not God himself but a deputy, a demiurge, a halfway god who created the world. He gave a name to that demiurge: "the logos". You may know that Greek word means "the Word" and you are going to see the relevance of this shortly. Philo said the world was created not so much by God, but by the logos – this demiurge, this somewhere in between.

We are not even sure if Philo thought of the logos as a person, or was simply personifying the force that created the world. We just don't know. We would have to ask him. Do you know what I mean by personifying? When a man talks about his new sports car as "she" – "She goes great!" That is personifying. It is not a person, but you are talking as if it is. So we are not sure whether he was personifying the logos or saying the logos was a person. But these are some of the things that were going on in Alexandria.

Let us look very quickly at the conflict between Greek thinking and Christianity. All that I have said so far happened before Christ came. After Christ came it was inevitable, as the Christian faith spread around the Mediterranean world, that there would be a head on encounter with Greek thinking. Of course for the first few decades, and possibly the first century or so, Christianity was protected by the fact that it was persecuted. Believers were regarded as different. They were outlaws. They were illegal, a *religio illicita*. They were not legally recognised as a religion; they were persecuted.

I don't need to go into all that, but hundreds of thousands of them had happen to them exactly what the people of many other places have experienced – they were killed for their faith. Of course that protected them in a sense from being unduly influenced by those who regarded them as enemies, and kept them at a distance. However, sooner or later the encounter was inevitable. Yes – the culture and the philosophy were all around them. The little churches grew up in the Graeco-Roman world.

There were two places I want to draw your attention to. The first is western Turkey. My wife and I had the privilege of going out for a week with a film crew and fifty people. We went around the seven churches of Asia, filming them, talking about them, studying the letters that Jesus wrote to those seven churches. I am amazed that people pay more attention to Paul's letters than Jesus' letters. Isn't that surprising? We have only got seven letters Jesus ever wrote to churches, and they are wonderful letters, but they are all in a tiny area. You can see the area clearly, not just on a map but from outer space. I have a satellite photograph of Turkey and there is a little green strip along the top, on the Black Sea coast. The rest is brown and dry except for a little circle in the southwest, which is bright green. That circle of green to this day covers the seven churches of Asia, or at least the remains of those seven cities.

It was a fabulously fertile, wealthy area with rivers running through. One of them was called the River Meander.

Did you ever hear of that? It has given its name to every river like that. These rivers produced fabulously fertile valleys. There was gold in there. That is where money was invented. King Croesus lived there and invented money to make exchange easier. Have you ever heard the saying, "Rich as Croesus"? Probably not, but there is such a proverb. Here in this area there is a fabulously concentrated example of Graeco-Roman culture. To walk down the main street in Ephesus and look even at the remains of the theatre, the library, the magnificent Greek architecture, is to realise that in this circle was concentrated the culture and the philosophy of the classical world.

It was not only a wealthy, cultured area, it was right on the main road from Europe to Africa and Asia. The road actually split and went around both sides of the little circle, joined up again, and on to India, China and Africa. It was a key area, and there were seven little churches there at the end of the first century AD.

The devil made that area his top priority. He actually had his headquarters there in a place called Pergamum. When Jesus wrote to the church at Pergamum he said, "I know where you reside because that is where Satan resides." Satan can't be in more than one place at once. He has a headquarters and at that time his headquarters was in western Turkey at Pergamum, on the top of the highest mountain that overlooked the town.

If you go to Pergamum today on the top of that mountain you will see theatres, a stadium, libraries; a most magnificent collection of culture is concentrated on the top of that hill. You have to go up a little winding road to the top – it is so steep. If you have been to Pergamum you will have seen that hill. Would you see the throne of Satan? No, you wouldn't, because it has been moved to Germany. If you want to see it now you have to go to the Pergamum Museum in Berlin because it was moved there, stone by stone by a German archaeologist. It was a gigantic armchair, a U-shaped temple. In the middle was an altar, and black smoke used to rise from that altar day and night. You could look up from the town below and see this great huge stone armchair with hundreds of Greek pillars, and the steps leading up to it. I have seen it in Berlin. The steps go up very high.

You can only see the foundation now. But that is where Satan's seat or throne was – his cathedra – in those days. That is why Jesus wrote to those seven churches. It was touch and go. If those seven little churches could survive there, the Church would survive anywhere. Or would they go under with all the culture and philosophy pressing them down? That is why Jesus wrote to those churches and no others. I have made a video of the letters he wrote, with all the shots of the towns themselves and the remains. Do get it. God is using that as prophetic word to the Church today. Somehow Jesus was saying to those churches, "You're giving in. There is idolatry; there is immorality even in your churches."

One of the most astonishing things which I point out in that video is that the distance of the churches from Satan's headquarters defined the problems they had. The two churches that were nearest Satan's headquarters were corrupted from the inside with idolatry and immorality. The two churches further away from Satan's headquarters were being attacked from the outside by Jewish people, whom Jesus calls "synagogues of Satan." But the two churches furthest away from Satan's headquarters – Laodicea and Ephesus – Satan wasn't bothering with at all. One of them had lost its first love and the other was simply neither cold nor hot, just lukewarm. It is fascinating to see that the problems the churches were having were in direct ratio to their distance from Satan's throne. Be that as it may – you must get the video and study it. And it is to those seven churches that Jesus revealed the future of godless civilisation. The rest of the book of Revelation is simply an unveiling of where godless civilisation finishes up. And he is saying: Don't go down with that. Come out of Babylon before her sins destroy you.

Now inevitably in the realm of thinking, the first question that would arise would be the person of our Lord Jesus Christ. If your brain has separated the physical from the spiritual, heaven from earth, eternal from the temporal, sacred from secular – if you are thinking like that, where do you put Jesus in your thinking? Which end of the ladder is he? Are you beginning to understand the problem?

Or is he in fact the Greek demiurge in the middle, the half and half? So it was in Ephesus, in the biggest city in that golden circle, that the first indications arise in your New Testament that people were beginning to force Jesus into a Greek framework, thinking that he couldn't be both; that he couldn't be right up there and right down here; that he couldn't be both God and man; that he couldn't be both spiritual and physical, but that he must be somewhere in between, neither fully divine nor fully human, like the Greek demiurge, somewhere halfway between. I am putting it very crudely, but basically this is what the Greek thinking about Jesus began to do.

It is not an unknown problem today. The Jehovah's Witness knocking at your door thinks the same way about Jesus. He is a Greek thinker about Jesus. He cannot accept that Jesus is fully God and fully man. So the apostle John, who was the only apostle still alive, the only one to die of old age, and who was living in Ephesus with Mary the mother of Jesus until she died (and you will see in the film, where I stand at the grave of the Apostle John, and just thank the Lord for that man). He wrote one Gospel and three letters to deal with that situation. The purpose of John's Gospel can be very simply stated. It was to tell people: you must go on believing that Jesus is fully human and fully divine. To emphasise his humanity, the shortest verse in John's Gospel (and in the Bible) is "Jesus wept" – at the grave of Lazarus. He was fully human.

In fact, Jesus is *more human* (if you can say that) in John's Gospel than the other three. But he is more clearly divine in the other three. John brings seven witnesses to bear that he is God, and seven miracles, more sensational than anything in Matthew, Mark and Luke, and seven statements "I am", which is God's name: "I am the bread of life"; "I am the light of the world"; "I am the good shepherd"; "I am the resurrection and the life"; "I am the true vine"; "I am the door"; "I am the way, the truth, and the life".... Sometimes it was just, "I am," by itself. John, in great daring, was puzzling: what do you call Jesus before he was born? Because he wasn't called Jesus before he was conceived; that is his human name. With a bold stroke of genius, he said, "He is the logos."

But the logos is not halfway between God and man. "In the beginning was the logos, and the logos was face to face with God, and the logos *was God.*" Not a demiurge; not halfway up the scale. He was *God*, and the logos was *made flesh* and lived among us. Do you see what John's Gospel is all about?

He is saying that he was right up there and he is right down here. He is fully God and fully man. He is the Logos who is both, not the logos who is in between.

I have been focusing on southwest Turkey. That is where the first great encounter took place and where Jesus himself stepped in with letters, and a revelation of the future, to try and hold those churches pure, and away from being swallowed up in the Graeco-Roman world. But now I want you to turn your attention to Africa, where I am afraid the battle was lost. The battle was won in southwestern Turkey and many Christians paid the price of martyrdom. Men like the Bishop of Smyrna, Polycarp, modern Izmir, but come with me first to the city of Alexandria, where Philo the Jewish scholar had lived. Now came Christian scholars to the same university, in particular two called Clement and Origen. They swallowed this same allegorical method of Bible study, this same not taking the Bible at face value, but trying to find a spiritual meaning behind it, some hidden code, some spiritual meaning. I call it "super-spirituality" because the Greeks did become super-spiritual. These Christian scholars followed Philo in this method, and many Christian preachers do today.

Let us take an example. Have you heard preachers talk about the water that flows (at the end of Ezekiel) that is first ankle deep, then knee deep, then waist deep – and use it as an allegory, even of the twentieth century? Well the first question I ask about Ezekiel's vision there is: does water mean water or something else? If you read it, you see that it clearly means water — H^2O. That is its simple plain meaning. This water actually flows in a geographical location. It flows in a valley, down towards the Dead Sea, and it reaches a specific place called Ein Gedi, and it fills the Dead Sea with fresh living water. Fishermen go fishing along the shores of the Dead Sea. It is a simple vision of what God could do and wanted to do: freshen up the Dead Sea. Hallelujah! Ah, but no, we must find an allegorical meaning! Well, I ask you, what is the allegorical meaning of Ein Gedi? I just think it means Ein Gedi. What is the allegorical meaning of fishermen? Oh evangelists – who said so?

Or let me take another example. After the resurrection Jesus said, "I'll meet you in Galilee," and disciples went north. They hung around for a few days and Jesus didn't appear, and Peter cannot sit still. So he says, "I'm going fishing." John says, "All right, I'll come with you." He might as well be doing something as nothing. So off they went, fishing, toiled all night, caught nothing. I have spent a night with fishermen on the Sea of Galilee; it is a wonderful experience. If you throw the net out you might get five fish, seven if you are lucky. So you keep throwing it. But they toiled all night and caught nothing. In the morning, the sun comes up and there's a man standing on the shore, and he tells them that they are doing it all wrong. You know, if ever you see a fisherman he is waiting for you to give him advice. He is waiting for someone to come and he says to them: "You're doing it all wrong. Try this and you'll get a catch." You try it with the next fisherman you see – they will be so grateful to you!

The man said, "Throw it that way, not this way." So they threw it that way and they got 153 fish in one throw. You wouldn't believe what preachers have tried to make that into. The favourite interpretation of 153 is: if you take the twelve apostles and square them you get 144, if you take the three persons of the Trinity and triple them you get nine, and 144 plus nine is 153. Therefore it is a symbol of the twelve apostles plus the Trinity. And that is the most sensible of the suggestions that have been made!

There have been dozens of allegorical meanings given to 153. I am going to give you the true meaning of 153. The true meaning is: that is an awful lot of fish. We start reading things into scripture, trying to find some hidden spiritual meaning. Let us just praise the Lord that is a lot of fish. Are you getting the message? We all do it. I am afraid Clement and Origen began to do it for the Christian Church. And of course you can make scripture mean anything you like.

But we must move along the African coast in a westward direction to what is now called Tunisia, to a little one-horse town. I am using that phrase advisedly because the town was called Hippo and that is the Greek word for horse, and "*potamus*" is the Greek word for river. So the horse of the river is called "Hippopotamus." But this was a city just called Hippo. There was a young man sent there to be bishop who is now the most famous man in church history. His name was Augustine.

Augustine was brought up in Italy where he was given a classical education in what was called "neo-Platonism", or the teaching of Plato brought up to date. But like most products of that culture, his body and his soul went different ways. When you divide a man up, that can happen. His soul studied philosophy and sought the good, but his body became promiscuous. He had a mistress and an illegitimate son whom he later abandoned. He was a bad boy, but of course they didn't believe that what you did with your body affected your soul. The two were quite distinct. But that was his life. He even joined a sect called the Manicheans, for whom physical matter was incurably evil. Of course, the way he lived, what he did with his body, he could believe that.

With this background he became convicted of sin, had contacts with a very saintly bishop, called Ambrose (Bishop of Milan) who wrote a song which you may have heard many times: "We praise thee O God: we acknowledge thee to be the Lord; All the earth doth worship thee: the Father everlasting...." Do you know it? The Te Deum. If you have read *The Confessions* of Augustine you know that he was converted quite dramatically and sat under the ministry of this saintly Bishop Ambrose. But he was chosen to become bishop of Hippo in what is now Tunisia, and he went there.

At first he preached a simple gospel, preached the Bible as it was, but then he began to preach against things and against people, and to write against them. Alas, you can trace what happened. The more he wrote against people and preached against them, the more his old thinking took over. I want to say, to put it very simply, that Augustine more than anybody else, recast the Christian faith in a Greek framework and has influenced the entire Church ever since. I am going to give you examples in Part 2. But Catholics look back to Augustine as their father in their thinking, and so do Protestants. Both Catholics and Protestants look back to this man as the greatest theologian of the Church.

Martin Luther was an Augustinian monk and so was brought up on Augustine. Calvin studied Augustine in Paris at the university, and his *magnum opus*, his huge volumes called *The Institutes of the Christian Religion*, have been described I think accurately as "systematic Augustinianism". I was brought up as a Methodist to think that the four great figures in the evangelical tradition were Paul, Augustine, Luther and Wesley. Then I met others who thought of Paul, Augustine, Luther and the Puritans rather than the Methodists. But Augustine appears in every family tree of every part of the Church. Everybody looks back to him and yet, I declare this sincerely, I believe he has done more damage to the Christian Church than any other man. I marvel at his conversion – that was wonderful. But to recast the Christian faith in neo-Platonic terms instead of Hebrew terms has been a disaster.

The Church has been pulling up its Hebrew roots both before and ever since. Easter was quickly separated from Passover. Whitsunday quickly separated from Pentecost, and Christmas moved months away from the Feast of Tabernacles. And as we pulled up our Jewish roots as a Church we put roots down into Greek philosophy, into Roman practice, and into pagan customs. Christmas has *nothing to do with Christ*. It was simply because a Pope sent another Augustine to Canterbury to convert those dreadful English. He wrote back to the Pope and said, "I can't wean them off their midwinter festival, their orgy of eating and drinking, when they sing carols and dance and for twelve days one elected man in every village can have sex with all the girls in the village. He is the lord of the Yuletide." (Think of: The Twelve days of Christmas, and "... my true love said to me" – and you still sing it. You haven't any idea what you're singing about).

The Pope wrote back and said, "If we can't lick 'em, join them. Bring the festival into Christ. Baptise it into our ritual" – and Christmas became a sacred cow. I have discovered the hard way. If you dare to criticise Christmas you are touching something so sacred, and yet it is nothing but a pagan festival that was brought in because people wouldn't give it up when they came to Christ.

So there was Augustine, and there was another figure, a man called Aquinas – his name was Thomas, but he came from Aquino in Italy so they called him Thomas Aquino, or Thomas Aquinas (c. 1225-1274). He didn't bring Plato into the Church, he brought in Aristotle. He brought in a natural theology based on reason. He was unlike Plato as Plato saw the spiritual world as the real world but Aristotle saw the natural world as the real world. He laid the foundations for science and for evangelical scepticism. There is a wonderful essay in a volume dedicated to John Stott on his eightieth birthday, showing how evangelicals go back to Aquinas and Aristotle and are sceptical about anything non-rational. So we are *all* affected, for better or worse, by this Greek influence.

The second Part is more interesting because we are going to look at some of the areas where our Christian thinking has been diverted from Hebrew thinking even today, and how to cure it in yourself.

PART TWO

I want to take five subjects of Christian belief and behaviour which have been profoundly affected from Augustine onwards without us realising. Number one, our bodies; Christians don't really know what to do with their bodies. We don't want to know about bodily functions. If we are good souls trapped in evil bodies, then the last thing we should talk about in church is our bodies or our bodily functions. There was a vicar once who said, "I'm going to show you that part of my body which causes me most temptations." There was a silence in the church and then he poked his tongue out! But he was wrong: the tongue doesn't cause you any problems at all. It is you who cause your tongue problems.

Do you say grace before you eat? I tend to give thanks for the first course and ask forgiveness for the second. But I was in a Christian home where there was father, mother, two children, and me sitting at the table – and I think it was roast lamb and mint sauce, which makes me drool anyway before I get to the table. The father said to me, "Would you please give thanks for us, Mr. Pawson?"

So I said, "Lord, I'm ready for this and it's ready for me, so thank you," and I opened my eyes and the father was looking at me in horror. "I thought we had a man of God here," you know? But I think a long prayer when you have got a hot meal in front of you is sacrilege. God has given us all things freely to enjoy. We are free to feast and we are free to fast.

Do you believe that our Lord Jesus Christ had to empty his bowels and bladder every day? You see, funnily enough, non-Christians have problems believing in the full deity of Christ, but I find most Christians have problems believing in the full humanity of Christ. He really is both. He is, was, and always will be, a full human being. In the Jewish book of prayer, there is a lovely prayer to pray when you go to the toilet. Now in Western congregations whenever I say that, there is a titter, if not a giggle; fancy mentioning that in church!

I go to many Christian toilets because I stay in Christian homes all over the world. A Christian loo usually has a pile of devotional books by the throne and there is a text on the wall, framed – all designed to keep my mind on spiritual things while I am in there. But the Jewish prayer is a beautiful prayer. It thanks the Lord that your body's working properly and it praises the Lord that you now feel better. You are relieved and you come out of the loo saying "Hallelujah!" If you don't understand that God is as concerned about what you do in the loo as what you do in church, you are Greek. He made your body. I'll tell you this: one of the humiliations of old age is when you can't control your bowels and bladder properly. You go back into nappies. It will happen to some of us and it can be very humiliating. If that does happen, you will wish that you had prayed when you went to the loo, and thanked him when it was working properly. Whenever I mention that in a Jewish congregation, they don't even smile. But of course, he is the Creator as well as the Redeemer. He made the physical world; he made my body. It is a concern to him.

Do you say grace before you make love? Why not? "For

what we are about to receive, may the Lord make us truly thankful" – does that sound incongruous to you? You see, ever since Augustine we can't handle sex. It was Augustine who said that sex, even in marriage, is lust, concupiscence, and from then on the idea got a hold that somehow celibacy is a holier state than matrimony. In fact, the entire church became celibate in its priesthood not long afterwards. That is totally contrary to Hebrew thinking, where a rabbi *must* be married and must experience love so that he understands it.

I remember being invited to preach in a unique open-air meeting in front of the Niagara Falls in Canada. It was the first time they had allowed a religious meeting right there. What a backcloth! There were three speakers – myself first, then a Roman Catholic priest, then a Pentecostal pastor. It was being televised to the whole of Canada and part of the US. I got up and said, I'd love to talk about what you can see behind me, because I know the man who made the Niagara Falls. His name's Jesus, and without him nothing was made that has been made, and he helped to make that. But I'm not going to talk about that. I'm going to talk about sex, and I want to tell you how much pleasure God gets out of sex."

There was a crowd of thousands, but you could have heard a pin drop. Many of them were church people, and they looked as if they had forgotten how they got into this world. But I said, "It was God who thought up sex, that exquisite pleasure. It was he who invented it. It was in the world long before sin was." I said, "When two young people pledge loyalty to each other publicly and go away on their honeymoon and seal that pledge in that exquisite pleasure, God is with them, and he is saying, 'I made that' – and he has pleasure in human love."

The Roman Catholic priest got up second, and said, "I'm not married, and I'm not likely to be, but I want to talk about honeymoons." The Pentecostal pastor got up third and he said, "You'll never believe this, but when I asked the Lord what to talk to you about, he said, 'Tell them about your honeymoon.'" We found out later that Niagara is the honeymoon capital of North America. There were hundreds of honeymoon couples listening to us, and all the hotels around had special suites for honeymoon couples.

Is all this incongruous? You see, since Augustine, we don't know what to do with our bodies, but my Bible says your body is the temple of the Holy Spirit. It is God's residence – your body is, not your soul. This leads to an extraordinary attitude to the sacraments. People don't believe that doing something with your body can have a spiritual effect, but that is what a sacrament is. Taking physical bread and physical wine into my body can have a profound spiritual effect both ways. It could judge me, and I could be sick and even die if I take it without discerning the body.

Washed in the water of baptism, just H_2O, what can that do for you? Well, there is a young man my wife and I know of. He was a Hell's Angel, and he had the devil tattooed on his body as a Hell's Angel. When he became a Christian, he knew he should be baptized, but he had noticed that when people were, their shirt went wet and became transparent and he didn't want people to see the devil on his body, so he went to a surgeon and said, "Can you remove that?"

The surgeon told him, "Yes, I can, but it will take a lot of money and a lot of time. We have to graft skin from your thigh." He said, "I don't have the money and I don't have the time." A friend of ours baptised him in a swimming pool in the back garden and he went down into the water to bury his past and wash away his sins, and when he came up out of the water the devil had gone – washed off his back or wherever it was. If you tell him that baptism is just a symbol, he will laugh you in the face.

Sacraments are physical events with profound spiritual

effect, because we are one – we are not separate body and soul, we are one being. At death we lose the body. Is that a positive or a negative thing? If you believe in the immortality of the soul, it is a positive thing. If you believe in the resurrection of the body, it is a negative thing: to lose your body and be "unclothed", as Paul put it. But the good news is we are going to have a new body. We are not going to go floating on as spirit on clouds. We are going to get a new body! I'm glad about that, because the new body is going to be like his glorious body, and I can't wait to be thirty-three again. In your eighties you begin to look forward to getting a new body. You see, if our business is just to save souls, we have missed it. We are to save whole people.

Secondly, let us move on to work, which I mentioned earlier. Work was a necessary evil to the Greeks. You had to do it to get enough money to have leisure, or better still, if you got enough money to become a gentleman of leisure and you didn't need to work again, which is why so many people are entering the lottery today. "You know, I wouldn't need to work." Live for leisure. Live for mental and spiritual activity. Even Christianity has become a kind of leisure activity, whereas the major thing that anybody has to do for the Kingdom of God is from Monday to Friday – his daily work. I have conferences for men regularly, all over the world now, and the first thing I want to teach men is that your daily job is your sacred vocation for the Lord, and how you do that is going to settle your future.

But we have a graded list of work: missionary is at the top rung; pastors and evangelists are a good number two, and then doctors and nurses, maybe teachers, taxi-drivers, computer operators. Do you know, without consciously doing it, we are teaching this all the time in church? We say, "If you will become a missionary, we'll pray for you regularly. We will put your photo in the church porch." Don't get me wrong in what I'm going to point out now, but I have visited missionaries overseas. They are living in a missionary village with a Christian hospital and a Christian school, a Christian population; and there is another member of their home church who is the only Christian on the shop floor at the factory where he works. Who needs more prayer? Who is in the front line? I look forward to the day when we put the photo of every member up in the porch and say, "This is their mission field. This is where they work. Pray for them."

But, you see, we have evaluated work; we have scaled it like the Greeks – spiritual work is top. We even have divided people. The whole Church divided people into clerical and lay; professional and amateur Christians. Some are real Christians, or we say, "These are real Christians—they live by faith, while these others just have a wage or a salary." Absolute rubbish – we all have to live by faith. A small businessman today, if he pays his debts on time, which is Christian duty, to keep his cash flow, he needs more faith than I have needed to live. He really does.

So we have divided people up into sacred work and secular work, faith work and non-faith work, clerical and lay, religious and non-religious. It has riddled the church through and through. Martin Luther did get one thing right. He said, "All work ranks the same to God." It is not what job you have, it is how you do your job that the Lord is most interested in. Billy Graham's wife had a notice above the kitchen sink: "Divine services held here three times a day." She had got it right.

We even dress some Christians differently from others. Clerical dress was never intended by the Lord Jesus. But I came across an amazing letter by no less than a Pope in 428 AD. He'd heard that a monk had been made Bishop of Arles in France and had started wearing special clothes. He wrote a stinging letter to him. He said, "Clergy should be different from other people, but by their learning and *not* their garments, by their mode of life and not by what they wear, by their purity of thought and not by their peculiarity of dress." Remember that letter was by a Pope, no less! It needs to be sent back to the Popes, I think, today.

Third example: I have looked at the example of what our attitude is to our body and our bodily functions—thoroughly Greek. I have looked at our attitude to work as Christians—thoroughly Greek. I now look at our attitude to Israel, God's ancient people. God gave Abraham a covenant and promised him two *physical* things: firstly, physical descendants, a people; secondly, a land, a place for those people to live – physical promises, and God has never withdrawn those promises.

Furthermore, even the New Testament says that the gifts of God to the patriarchs are irrevocable, and they are still physical. The land is still a physical land and it still belongs to the Jewish people. The Jews are still a physical people and they are still the brothers of Jesus, and they are still beloved by God for the patriarchs' sake. They are not saved until they believe in their own Messiah, but they are beloved. They are his chosen people.

He promised them blessings when they were obedient, and most of those blessings were physical: health – none of the diseases of Egypt touching them; fertility – plenty of rain on their fields. But he also promised curses on their disobedience which were also physical – sickness, flood, drought; most of the miracles in the Old Testament, indeed I think all of them, were physical miracles. There was the dividing of the Red Sea. The kingdom of Israel was physical, the king was physical, but we have made the new covenant with Israel entirely spiritual. The Church has gone in for what is called "replacement theology" and called the Church "Israel", which the New Testament never does; not even the "new Israel", though that is one of the most common phrases used in the Christian church today, as if God is finished with his physical people and he is only interested now in his spiritual people.

Therefore, there is no use mentioning the land of Israel in the current Middle East situation, because it is now irrelevant. The main concern in the Middle East is simply how to get peace, as if the land has been taken back again from God's people. Now of course they don't hold it unconditionally. I believe their *ownership* of the land is unconditional, but their *occupation* is conditional, not least on the way they treat strangers within the land. But nevertheless, God's physical promise still stands to his physical people of a physical land. The word "Israel" is used over seventy times in the New Testament, not once of the Christian Church.

It is still his physical people to whom he made a physical promise. Well I move over that, but here is why the majority of the Church in this country would not be interested in an olive tree meeting. They just wouldn't be. The Church, the spiritual Israel, has replaced the physical Israel. You see, once again spiritual is of more value than physical – it is Greek thinking, and that is not to touch the anti-Semitism.

But I want to come to two major issues finally. The first is the earth and its future. We live by faith, hope and love. "Now abideth faith, hope and love" – but the weakest of these is hope. I find that Christians are in total confusion about hope for the future. I have asked congregation after congregation over the last three years to vote on this question: "Do you believe the next century will be better than this, worse than this, or much the same?" Which do you think the vote is? Eighty-five percent of Christian people put their hands up for worse. There is a mood of pessimism. We came into the twentieth century in a mood of optimism. The word on everybody's lips was "progress". Now the word on everybody's lips is "survival". There are many voices telling us we won't even survive another hundred years. 2040 is the date that many computer programmes are giving as the date beyond which human life will become impossible. If population trends, food resources and fuel resources continue as they are, then 2040 is the date they are talking about for the end – pessimism.

Now Christians are people of hope. Unfortunately, the English word hope means "wish". "I hope it's going to be fine tomorrow." "I hope I'll win the national lottery." What people mean is, "I'm not at all sure; in fact, I'm very unsure", whereas the Greek word for hope in the New Testament, "*elpis*" means that which I am *absolutely certain* is going to happen. It is an anchor to the soul when the storm hits.

So what do we hope for the future? I am talking about our hope for this earth, this world. What is your Christian hope for this world? Is it ever going to be a world of peace? Well it doesn't look like it, does it? We could be in World War Three. It was a little dispute in the Balkans that set off World War One. Now Russia is uttering threats; who knows? The thing just seems to gather like a snowball – more and more people get more and more involved, and we ordinary people just read the newspapers. What can we do? Our leaders seem hell-bent on escalation.

Do you think there will ever be multilateral disarmament? Do you think there will ever be world peace? What is your hope? I am absolutely certain there is going to be, because Jesus is coming back to earth. That is the focus of Christian hope in the New Testament. He is coming back here bodily, physically. He is coming back! There are two things that have now almost totally disappeared from Christian teaching about the future, and they were once very prominent. Christ is returning to earth. You do believe that, don't you? Do you believe that you are returning to earth after you are dead?

You are not so sure about that, you know. You believe you are coming back here to this old earth to live again, a second time here? That's the Christian hope for the future, because God will bring with him all those who have fallen asleep in Christ Jesus.

I have only been to and spoken at four funerals in the last few years: my mother-in-law (98); my daughter (36); my sister (cancer); my brother-in-law (cancer). When I said "They'll be back", people looked at me as if I was teaching reincarnation. They will stand on this earth again. When Jesus stands on this earth, they will. I told you I am looking forward to getting a brand-new body, but I won't get it in heaven. I don't need a body up there. I shall need a body when I get back here because you can't live in this world without a body. That is where you are going to get your new body. This is where the resurrection of the body takes place – here, not up there.

The Bible is thoroughly down-to-earth in its hope for the future, but why is Christ coming back? What is he coming back to do? Why is he bringing all the dead Christians back as well? Why are we all coming back here? Some people seem to think we're only going to stay for two minutes, just long enough to get our new body – and off. Other people, quite wrongly, say every Sunday at communion in the Nicene Creed, or even in the Apostles' Creed, "That from thence he shall come again to judge the quick and the dead." He is not coming back to earth to judge the quick and the dead. He is not going to judge the quick and the dead until the earth is gone.

In my Bible it is quite clear that when we appear before the great white throne the earth has passed away already. So he is not coming back to judge. Then what is he coming back for? Just to take us all back again? Why bring millions of Christians back from heaven to earth just to go back to heaven again? That seems a little bit of a waste of energy.

Well how long is he coming back for? He was here thirty-three years the first time. How long is he coming back for the second? For four hundred years the Church was utterly clear in its hope of the future for this world and that hope was, to quote Papias, the ancient Bishop of Hierapolis: "We believe that Christ… in the corporeal reign of Christ on earth", meaning the bodily reign of Christ on earth for a thousand years. I am amazed – the word millennium used to be the Church's preaching, now everybody else is using the word except Christians. Isn't that incredible?

My Bible tells me quite simply that he is coming back to take over world government for a thousand years here, and we are coming back to share it with him and to reign here. It says, "Blessed is he, he's redeemed with his own blood, from every kindred and tribe and tongue and people, men for God and they shall reign on the earth." Not up there; down here. The meek will inherit the earth one day. Jesus said it would happen – not heaven, the *earth*. When we were getting up to the year two thousand, everybody was talking about the millennium, but they were talking about the wrong millennium.

A week after the year 2000, things were exactly the same as they were a week before. But *the* millennium – what a hope for the future, that one day the devil will be kicked out. The reason why we cannot have the kingdom on earth established before Jesus gets back is that we can't get rid of the prince of this world, the devil. You can't get rid of him and neither can I. We can rescue his victims and get them out of his kingdom into the Kingdom of Christ. The devil is far too clever for you – too powerful. He will only be kicked out when Jesus gets back, and then the world will have a Christian government at last.

You may have sung the hymn "Jesus shall reign where e'er

the sun, doth his successive journeys run", or my favourite hymn as a boy: "Sing we the king who is coming to reign, glory to Jesus, the lamb that was slain. Life and salvation his empire shall bring, joy to the nations when Jesus is king!" Do you believe it? He is coming back to rule, to reign, and if there is one thing I long to hear the Church announcing it is that Jesus is coming back to reign for a thousand years here, on this old earth. You will see then "the nations beat their swords into ploughshares and their spears into pruning hooks. And nation shall not lift up sword against nation; neither shall they learn war anymore."

That half a text is outside the United Nations building in New York on a block of granite, but the other half says "when the Lord reigns in Zion". *He*, Jesus, will settle the disputes among the nations, and *then* they will beat their swords into ploughshares.

Oh, but we can allegorise it, can't we? We can allegorise all the promises, such as that the wolf will lie down with the lamb and the lion will eat straw like the ox. Do you believe that, or do you think we should allegorise it? The wolf and the lamb should be the vicar and the churchwarden getting on well together. That is how we allegorise it away. And "the desert shall blossom like a rose." Why shouldn't it? The Sahara was once a garden. Why can't it be a garden again? Do you see what I mean by taking scripture in its plain, simple sense?

The millennium has almost disappeared, and do you know the man responsible? Augustine. In his early ministry he preached that Jesus was coming back for a thousand years to reign on earth, and that is what all the Church believed and preached until then. There is not a trace of any other view. Nobody discussed "are you amillennial, premillennial, or postmillennial?" A friend of mine said, "That's a-pre-post-erous question!" We have got into all these different views since Augustine. He taught the Church what is called postmillennialism – that we are in the millennium already. Well, frankly, if this is the millennium, and the devil is supposed to be bound, sealed and locked up in a dungeon so he can't deceive anybody anymore, I want to know who is carrying on his business!

I am deadly serious. I wrote this book to call the Church back to the message it preached for the first four hundred years. But Augustine could not believe that Jesus would come back physically to a physical world and rule physically. It was all much too physical. It wasn't spiritual enough and he persuaded a Council in the year 431 in Ephesus – and I have stood in the ruins of the church where this was decided – they condemned belief in the millennium as heresy. That was an official council of the Church. That is why you have never heard about it in most churches; why Revelation 20 is either completely ignored or totally twisted around to mean something else. It is treated allegorically, but what a glorious gospel to preach: Jesus is coming back to reign and this world is going to see what it can be like under a Christian government. And the responsibility you have in that millennium will depend on how you do your daily job now.

I was preaching on the millennium recently. A man came up to me afterwards and was so excited, he said, "David, for the first time I can relate my faith to my job."

I asked him, "Why? What's your job?"

"I'm in charge of de-polluting the rivers of England," he replied. "We've even got salmon in the Thames again." He continued, "I know from Revelation that the rivers and the oceans are going to be dreadfully polluted before the end. When Jesus comes back to reign, he'll need someone to clean up the rivers for him, and I want that job! I'm going to learn as much as I can about it."

Suddenly the man saw that his daily work was a preparation for the millennium; that he was going to reign with Christ.

We are going to rule the nations with a rod of iron. That doesn't mean with cruelty. It means undemocratically, a benevolent dictatorship of a Christian government. One day the television will be in Christian hands, the banks will be in Christian hands, the courts will all be in Christian hands. Can you imagine it? Brothers and sisters, we can't even run the church properly now. We had better get in training.

The other thing that has disappeared from Christian preaching about the future is the new earth. Even beyond Christ's reign on the old earth, there's a brand new earth. When people ask me what my job is, I say I am in the recycling business. They are always pleased. "What do you recycle – metal, paper, bottles?"

"No – people, because they are the cause of pollution."

God is in the business of recycling people, because one day he is going to recycle the entire universe, he is going to make a new earth. I love preaching on the new earth, but whenever I do so, somebody accuses me of being a Jehovah's Witness.

I was in Sydney, Australia, and I preached on the new earth and I said, "In the new earth, there will be no sun, no sea and no sex." Not a single "hallelujah!" They all looked glum. We were about five miles from Bondi Beach, and they looked as if they wanted to get out of the meeting and get down to Bondi Beach where you can get all three in good measure. You won't even miss any of them. A new earth? Did you think we are going to go to heaven and live with God forever? No, heaven is only a temporary waiting room between death and resurrection, then you come back here to the old earth first, and then into a brand new one.

Do you know what's going to happen then? God is

going to move house. It is God who is moving, not us, and he is coming to earth to live with us. That is the last page of the Bible: not up there but down here. The angel says, "Behold! Look! The dwelling place of God is with men." Not the dwelling place of men is with God, it is the other way around. He is coming down here and the new Jerusalem is coming down out of heaven – here – and the Lamb will be here and God will be here. It actually says we shall see his face – not Jesus' face, God's face. You are going to see it, which brings me to the final point.

The Greek view of God is so far removed from the Hebrew. The Greek gods were only too human and too weak. If you study Greek mythology, you will find out they were only too human, so the philosophers lifted God right away from the human sphere, right out into a timeless eternity, away from emotions, away from change and decay, away from time and space, in another world altogether – a static God, not a dynamic one; a God who had attributes, rather than actions; a God who was omnipresent, everywhere; a God who was omnipotent, who could do anything; a God who was omniscient, who knew everything, but in my Bible, God is none of those three things.

He is everywhere he chooses to be. He is not *everywhere*, and he is already creating a place called hell where he will *not* be. And God is not omnipotent. There are many things God can't do, powerful though he is, almighty though he is. I made a list of thirty-one things that he could not do – a bit shocked to find out how many I could. The first thing I wrote down was he cannot tell a lie, cannot break a promise. But here is one thing I wrote down: he cannot change the past. God himself cannot change the past. He can change the future, not the past. But the Greeks developed a static God who was totally without emotions and who never changed in any particular. He was immutable. Have you heard these words? But my Bible is about a God who can change his mind, and who does, and even does so in response to pleading prayer. Moses managed to get God to change his mind. Amos did the same thing. You read it. And I don't find a God without feelings and emotions, I find a God who can be sad and angry and happy, who can rejoice over us with singing and even whistling – a God who whistles; and a God who is described as having a nose, nostrils, a mouth, eyes, ears, a face, hand, fingers, arm, legs, feet, even bowels and kidneys, and even sperm. They talk of God as if he is just a human being in the Bible. They know perfectly well he is Spirit and doesn't have a body. But what they are saying is: if you want to imagine what God is like then think of yourself.

Even your own body tells you what God is like. We are made in his image, even our body is, and we can do with the body what he can do without a body. You can see; so can he. You can smell; so can he. You can talk; so can he. You can hear; so can he. You can walk; so can he. You can whistle; so can he. That is the Hebrew view of God. But the Greeks thought that was a very primitive, simplistic, childish view of God. They gave the term anthropomorphism to thinking that God is like a human being. But that is the very best way you *can* think of God, because that is what he is like. This Greek god who is a changeless, immutable, distant, static god made eternal decrees. He didn't make temporal decisions, whereas the God of my Bible changes his decisions in response to human beings. He is in a dynamic relationship.

Think of the potter and the clay in Jeremiah. Have you learned the lesson of the potter and the clay? Jeremiah went to the potter's house and he saw a potter with a lump of clay on the wheel, and he tried to make it into a beautiful vase as he pumped the wheel. He tried to make this lovely vase, but the clay wouldn't run in his hands. So the potter put it in a lump, pushed it on the wheel and made a crude, thick pot of the clay. And God said, "Jeremiah, who decided what the clay became, the potter or the clay?" Now think that through. Who decided what the clay became? The answer is the clay. And God said: "Israel is like that. I wanted to make her a beautiful vessel, full of my mercy. But they wouldn't run in my hands and I'm going to make them a crude pot full of my judgment; but if they change their mind and repent, then I will change my mind and I will repent and I'll make them a beautiful vase again." But it is the clay that is deciding.

The next day, "Jeremiah, go back to the potter and look at that jar again." Now he found it, and now it was hard. It had baked in the sun, and he was told to take it out and throw it down into the Valley of Gehenna just outside Jerusalem and smash it to pieces, because by now it couldn't change its mind. It had become too hard. "Jeremiah, have you learned the lesson of the clay?" The clay can decide whether God makes it a vessel of mercy or judgment. But there comes a point where the clay has become too hard to change. That is the relationship between God and human beings. You may have sung the chorus "You are the potter; I am the clay", as if it is all up to you, God, what you make of me. No, it is not. It is up to you what you let him make you.

It was Augustine who developed a doctrine of pre-destination which is predetermination, and said that we are saved if God has made an eternal decree – way up there in eternity, way removed from time and space – and made a decree that you will be saved and your next-door neighbour will not be. Ever since then, predestination has been falsely preached in a *Greek* sense, which is not the biblical view of predestination at all. Find that in my book *Once Saved, Always Saved?* because, again, if God has made an eternal decree that you be saved and go to heaven, then there is nothing you can do to change that, and you will never be lost – once saved, always saved. But I question whether once saved, always saved is Bible teaching. God is not in that kind of relationship with you. He doesn't force anyone. He is not an almighty giant who treats us like puppets. This changeless, immutable god who makes eternal decrees is not the Hebrew God. The Hebrew God listens to prayers and says, "All right then, I hear your prayer. I won't destroy you. You change your mind and I'll change mine." What a God – a God you can influence through prayer! But in Greek you can't influence God. He is way above it all and you just must say "Your will be done." That is Islam; that is Insha'Allah. That is not the Hebrew God.

How can we avoid being 'Greeced'? How can we avoid being caught up in this Greek thinking which is riddling the Church through and through? I hope you have been able to recognise some of this just through the examples I have given you. Well, there is a negative and a positive side. The negative side is to be aware that this has happened. You need constantly to be alert when you are hearing Greek thinking instead of Jewish, Hebrew thinking. But there is a positive thing you can do, and this is the real answer. Soak yourself in the Bible. It is a Hebrew book, and if you pay more attention to other books, magazines and TV programmes, and more of that goes into your brain than biblical thinking, then you will inevitably become Greek, because that is our culture. If you soak yourself in the Bible, and particularly the Old Testament, that is the only protection we have against the Greek pressures of the world around us. But a recent survey of evangelical Christians in England revealed that three quarters of evangelical Christians are not reading their Old Testament. They may occasionally dip into it, but they are not soaking their mind in it.

Paul says: "Don't be a chameleon, be a caterpillar" (Romans 12:2). If you don't believe me, look it up. It is slightly different in your version. He says, "Don't let the world around you colour your thinking" – because that is what happens to the chameleon. Put him on red, he turns red; put him on blue, he turns blue. If you want to kill him, put him on tartan, then he explodes! So many people take their thinking from other people, even from the preachers they listen to, instead of getting into the Word themselves. Be a caterpillar. Paul actually says, "Have your mind metamorphised" – that is the word he uses in the Greek, and the caterpillar goes through a process of metamorphosis. An ugly little thing is a caterpillar, but a caterpillar is developing the most beautiful colours inside – not taking his colours from anywhere else, producing them from the inside, and one day those wings burst out, and the colour is seen. Don't be a chameleon. Don't take your thinking from around you. Be a caterpillar. Let the colour of your thinking come from the inside, but let the Spirit and the scripture colour you.

Soak yourself in the God of Israel. Study the Jewish people. Try and have some Jewish friends to help you read *their Bible*, because it is not ours, it is theirs. I have just found the more Hebrew you become in your thinking, the more you spot the Greek thinking, the more you notice it, and it worries you that there is so much inside the Church. Our roots are in Israel, not ancient Greece. Our faith is in the olive tree, which is Israel. We are wild olives, grafted into their roots. We draw our sap from their roots. Our thinking is to be Hebrew, for there is only one God, and he is not the god of Greece, he is the God of Israel.

> "How odd of God to choose the Jews;
> but odder still for those who choose
> the Jewish God and spurn the Jews."

ABOUT DAVID PAWSON

A speaker and author with uncompromising faithfulness to the Holy Scriptures, David brings clarity and a message of urgency to Christians to uncover hidden treasures in God's Word.

Born in England in 1930, David began his career with a degree in Agriculture from Durham University. When God intervened and called him to become a Minister, he completed an MA in Theology at Cambridge University and served as a Chaplain in the Royal Air Force for three years. He moved on to pastor several churches, including the Millmead Centre in Guildford, which became a model for many UK church leaders. In 1979, the Lord led him into an international ministry. His current itinerant ministry is predominantly to church leaders. David and his wife Enid currently reside in the county of Hampshire in the UK.

Over the years, he has written a large number of books, booklets, and daily reading notes. His extensive and very accessible overviews of the books of the Bible have been published and recorded in *Unlocking the Bible*. Millions of copies of his teachings have been distributed in more than 120 countries, providing a solid biblical foundation.

He is reputed to be the "most influential Western preacher in China" through the broadcast of his best-selling *Unlocking the Bible* series into every Chinese province by Good TV. In the UK, David's teachings are often broadcast on Revelation TV.

Countless believers worldwide have also benefited from his generous decision in 2011 to make available his extensive audio video teaching library free of charge at www.davidpawson.org and we have recently uploaded all of David's video to a dedicated channel on www.youtube.com

TAKE A LOOK AT YOUTUBE
www.youtube.com/user/DavidPawsonMinistry

THE EXPLAINING SERIES
BIBLICAL TRUTHS SIMPLY EXPLAINED

If you have been blessed reading this book, there are more available in the series. Please register to download more booklets for free by visiting
www.explainingbiblicaltruth.global

Other booklets in the *Explaining* series will include:
The Amazing Story of Jesus
The Resurrection: *The Heart of Christianity*
Studying the Bible
Being Anointed and Filled with the Holy Spirit
New Testament Baptism
How to study a book of the Bible: Jude
The Key Steps to Becoming a Christian
What the Bible says about Money
What the Bible says about Work
Grace – *Undeserved Favour, Irresistible Force
or Unconditional Forgiveness?*
Eternally secure? – *What the Bible says about being saved*
De-Greecing the Church – The impact of Greek thinking
on Christian beliefs
Three texts often taken out of context:
Expounding the truth and exposing error
The Trinity
The Truth about Christmas

They will also be avaiable to purchase as print copies from:
Amazon or **www.thebookdepository.com**

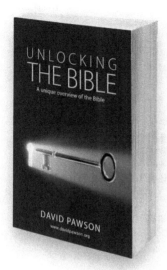

UNLOCKING
THE BIBLE

A unique overview of both the Old and New Testaments, from internationally acclaimed evangelical speaker and author David Pawson. *Unlocking the Bible* opens up the Word of God in a fresh and powerful way. Avoiding the small detail of verse by verse studies, it sets out the epic story of God and his people in Israel. The culture, historical background and people are introduced and the teaching applied to the modern world. Eight volumes have been brought into one compact and easy to use guide to cover both the Old and New Testaments in one massive omnibus edition. *The Old Testament: The Maker's Instructions* (The five books of law); *A Land and A Kingdom* (Joshua, Judges, Ruth, 1&2 Samuel, 1&2 Kings); *Poems of Worship and Wisdom* (Psalms, Song of Solomon, Proverbs, Ecclesiastes, Job); *Decline and Fall of an Empire* (Isaiah, Jeremiah and other prophets); *The Struggle to Survive* (Chronicles and prophets of exile); *The New Testament: The Hinge of History* (Mathew, Mark, Luke, John and Acts); *The Thirteenth Apostle* (Paul and his letters); *Through Suffering to Glory* (Hebrews, the letters of James, Peter and Jude, the Book of Revelation). Already an international bestseller.

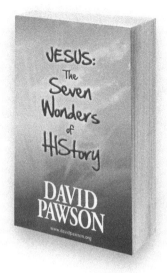

JESUS:
THE SEVEN
WONDERS
OF HISTORY

This book is the result of a lifetime of telling 'the greatest story ever told' around the world. David re-told it to many hundreds of young people in Kansas City, USA, who heard it with uninhibited enthusiasm, 'tweeting' on the internet about 'this cute old English gentleman' even while he was speaking.

Taking the middle section of the Apostles' Creed as a framework, David explains the fundamental facts about Jesus on which the Christian faith is based in a fresh and stimulating way. Both old and new Christians will benefit from this 'back to basics' call and find themselves falling in love with their Lord all over again.

OTHER TEACHINGS
BY DAVID PAWSON

For the most up to date list of David's Books
go to: **www.davidpawsonbooks.com**

To purchase David's Teachings
go to: **www.davidpawson.com**